ATLAS OF WORLD FAITHS

ISLAM

Cath Senker

A⁺

Smart Apple Media

This book has been published in cooperation with
Arcturus Publishing Limited.

Series concept: Alex Woolf
Editor and picture researcher: Alex Woolf
Designer: Simon Borrough
Cartography: Encompass Graphics
Consultant: Douglas G. Heming

Picture credits:
Corbis: cover (Christine Osborne), 5 (Art Archive/
Alfredo Dagli Orti), 6 (Kazuyoshi Nomachi), 8 (Hanan
Isachar), 12 (Archivo Iconografico, S.A.), 14 (Kevin
Fleming), 16 (Nik Wheeler), 19 (Kerim Okten/epa), 21
(Yann Arthus-Bertrand), 22 (Arthur Thévenart), 24
(David Ball), 26 (Daniel Lainé), 29 (Bettmann), 31
(Marc Garanger), 32 (Reuters), 35 (Baldev), 36–37
(Bettmann), 39 (Patrick Chauvel/Sygma), 40 (Ricki
Rosen).
World Religions Photo Library: 11.

Library of Congress Cataloging-in-Publication Data

Senker, Cath.
Islam / by Cath Senker.
p. cm. – (Atlas of world faiths)
Includes index.
ISBN 978-1-59920-055-2
1. Islam—History. 2. Islamic empire--History. I. Title. II.
Series.

BP50.S46 2007
297.09—dc22   2007007620

9 8 7 6 5 4 3 2 1

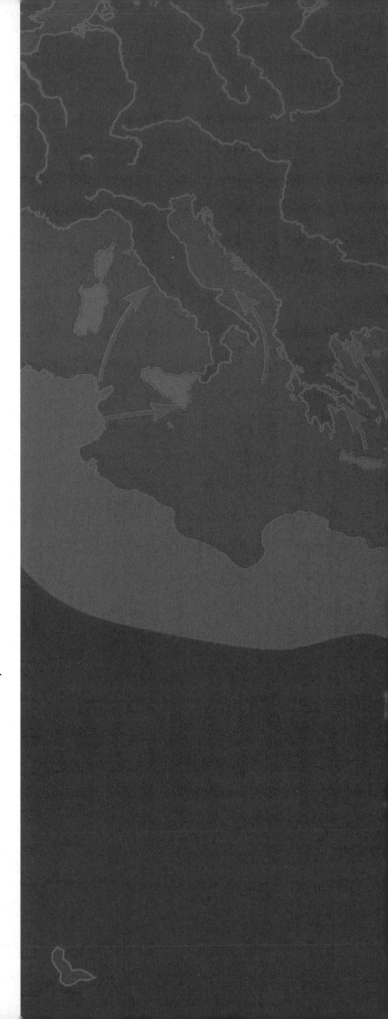

CONTENTS

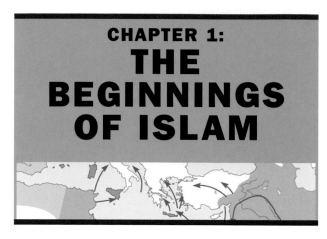

CHAPTER 1:
THE BEGINNINGS OF ISLAM

Islam was born in the harsh desert environment of sixth-century Arabia. Many of the Arabs, the inhabitants of the Arabian Peninsula, followed a nomadic existence—they moved from place to place with their herds. Others cultivated the land with the little water that was available, while a minority lived in towns. All people looked to their clan, or tribe, for protection.

The region was influenced by several religious traditions. The Byzantine Empire was the most important Christian empire in the region, and

Arabia before the coming of Islam, and the dominant empires of the region.

Christianity also was influential in southern Arabia. In the Sasanian Empire, based in Persia (Iran), a religion called Zoroastrianism was practiced. Throughout the region, there were also small Jewish communities.

Most Arabs believed in a creator god called Allah and various lesser deities to whom they turned for help in times of need. The center of religious life was the Ka'ba in the city of Mecca. The Ka'ba was a stone around which a sanctuary was built. It was said that the gods resided there. Pilgrims from around the peninsula came to worship the deities at the Ka'ba.

In the late sixth century, the Quraish was the dominant clan in Mecca. The Quraish controlled the Ka'ba and made money by charging pilgrims a fee for the right to worship at the sacred site. Many people grew resentful of the wealth of the Quraish.

Muhammad
Born in 570 CE, Muhammad was a member of the Quraish clan. After becoming an orphan, he was taken in by his grandfather and then by his uncle Abu Talib, a wealthy merchant. Muhammad grew up to be a trustworthy and hardworking assistant to Abu Talib. When he was about 25 years old, he married a wealthy widow named Khadijah.

A spiritual man, Muhammad spent much time in solitude. According to tradition, one night, when he was about 40 years old, Muhammad awoke to find himself overpowered by a presence that gripped his body. He found himself speaking the first words of a new scripture in beautiful Arabic poetry. He realized that Allah had chosen him to be his Prophet, or messenger. After two years of receiving revelations, Muhammad started preaching. He started a new religion called Islam, which means "submission" or "obedience" to the will of God. The Prophet gained followers, who later became known as Muslims (people who follow Islam).

Muhammad's main message was that there was one true God and that after people died, they would be rewarded or punished by God, depending on whether or not they had been good in their lives. His followers' first duty was to God rather than to their family or tribe. The Prophet taught that all people should be respected, including women and slaves (who were often badly treated) and that the wealthy should share their riches with the poor.

The hegira
The wealthy Quraish did not like Muhammad's message. After 619, when Abu Talib died, Muhammad no longer had a protector, and his new community was persecuted in Mecca. In 622, Muhammad and his followers moved to the town of Yathrib.

This scroll fragment is from a Qur'an dating to the eighth or ninth century.

THE QUR'AN AND HADITH

Muhammad's followers memorized the revelations he had received. After his death, the revelations were written down to form a book called the Qur'an, which means "recitation" (saying aloud). The Qur'an contains guidance on lawful and unlawful behavior for Muslims, as well as stories of the Jewish and Christian prophets who came before Muhammad. It explains the religious duties of a Muslim. During the first century CE, after Muhammad's death, reports of the Prophet's words and actions were collated in collections known as Hadith, or sayings.

ISLAM

The migration to Yathrib came to be known as the hegira (also called the hijra). Such was the significance of this event in the history of Islam that the year in which it occurred—622—became the first year of the Muslim calendar. Muhammad and his followers were welcomed in Yathrib, and from then on, the town was known as Madinat al-Nabi (City of the Prophet), or simply Medina.

Radical reforms In Medina, Muhammad was able to implement many reforms. He created a new kind of community called the Umma. To be a member of a traditional community, or tribe, a person had to be born into it. By contrast, anyone could join the Umma simply by saying the shahada, the Muslim profession of faith.

Muhammad was the absolute leader of the Umma. He declared every person's life equal, so that harming an orphan was as serious as harming a rich man. He outlawed usury (charging interest on loans) because

This modern photo shows pilgrims during evening prayers at the Prophet's Mosque in Medina.

high interest payments affected the poorest the most. Everyone had to give money to charity. This was called zakat. The amount people paid depended on what they could afford, and the money was distributed to the neediest. Muhammad also gave rights to women for example, allowing them to inherit property. The Qur'an says that men should take care of women but stresses equality of the sexes in the eyes of Allah.

THE FIVE PILLARS OF ISLAM

Since the beginning of Islam, Muslims have followed these practices:
1. They state the shahada, their belief in God.
2. Muslims pray five times a day. On Fridays, they gather at the mosque, the place for communal worship.
3. During the Muslim month of Ramadan, they fast during daylight hours.
4. At the end of Ramadan, all Muslims give zakat, one-fortieth of their wealth, to the poor.
5. All Muslims try to make the hajj (pilgrimage) to Mecca at least once in their lifetime.

Allah offers forgiveness and a great reward,
For men who surrender to Him, and women who
surrender to Him,
For men who believe, and women who believe,
For men who obey, and women who obey,
For men who speak the truth, and women who
speak the truth…

Qur'an 33:35

The Quraish regarded Muhammad's new society as
a threat to their authority and were determined to defeat
it. Over the next few years, there were battles between
the Quraish, based in Mecca, and the Muslims in
Medina. In 630, the Prophet conquered Mecca and its
people accepted his faith. Two years later, Muhammad
died. The Umma was then ruled in turn by four caliphs
(successors): Abu Bakr, Umar, Uthman, and Ali. Each of

them was appointed by the Muslim community. The
caliphs rapidly conquered further territory to create an
Islamic empire. By 644, the Muslims controlled Arabia,
Syria, Palestine, Egypt, and the former Persian Empire.

The Umayyads There was conflict within the
Umma. Uthman (ruled 644–656) was criticized for
appointing members of his clan, known as the
Umayyads, to important positions. He was assassinated
by Muslim soldiers who wanted Ali, the son-in-law of
Muhammad, to be the new caliph. But not all Muslims
accepted Ali's rule. The new Umayyad leader, Muawiya,
opposed Ali, but Ali would not fight him. A group of
rebels, the Kharijites, were angry with Ali for refusing to
fight and murdered him in 661. Muawiya then
appointed himself as caliph.

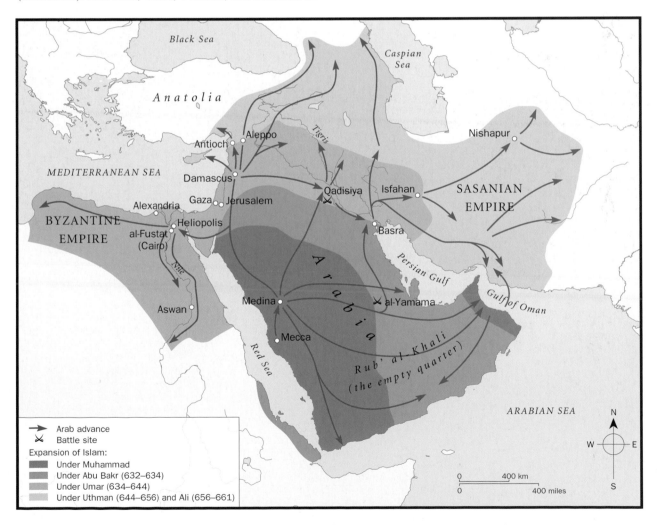

The expansion of Islam under Muhammad and the first four caliphs.

THE SUNNI–SHIA SPLIT

Two distinct forms developed within Islam. Some Muslims believed that the leadership should remain in the Prophet's family and that Ali should have been the successor to Muhammad. They became known as the shiat Ali—the Party of Ali. Two of Ali's grandsons survived the massacre in Karbala, and the Shia imamate (spiritual leadership) passed down through them. Today, most Shia Muslims believe there have been 12 Imams (leaders) and that the last Imam will return to restore justice on Earth.

However, the majority of Muslims thought that the best person for the job should become leader and that Muhammad did not intend to start a family line of rulers. They became known as Sunnis because they regarded themselves as the true followers of the Sunna—the customs of the Prophet.

Muawiya established the Umayyad dynasty, which lasted until 750. He ruled the Muslim lands from his new capital in Damascus, Syria. However, the struggle for control of the Islamic empire did not end there. Muawiya appointed his son Yazid as his successor, but Muslims still loyal to Ali believed that Ali's son Hussain should be caliph. Hussain led a small band of supporters to fight Yazid. In 681, Yazid's vast Umayyad forces surrounded Hussain's group in Karbala (in modern-day Iraq) and killed most of them.

The Dome of the Rock mosque in Jerusalem displays quotations from the Qur'an proclaiming the unity of God. It was built as a shrine over a rock that is believed to be the place where the Prophet Muhammad rose to heaven.

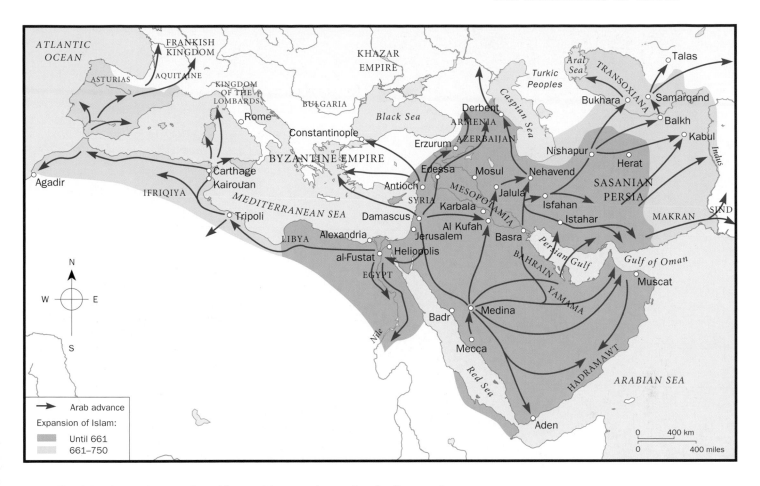

The Islamic empire continued its rapid expansion under the Umayyads.

The Umayyads experienced further revolts between 683 and 685 by the Shia, or those loyal to Ali, and the Kharijites, among others. But Abd al-Malik (ruled 685–705) reasserted Umayyad control. He replaced Persian as the official language of the empire with Arabic and introduced Islamic coinage. Under his rule, the Dome of the Rock mosque in Jerusalem was completed. It was the first major Islamic monument and a symbol of the confidence of the new religion. Under Abd al-Malik's son, al-Walid I (reigned 705–715), the Umayyad Empire reached its greatest extent. Muslim armies conquered territories beyond the Arabian Peninsula, including Iran, North Africa, and part of Spain.

Debates As the Islamic empire spread, there were debates over its nature. From the start of the empire's expansion, the Arab conquerors had kept themselves apart from the subject peoples, living in garrison cities (cities with strong military defenses). Non-Arabs who had converted to Islam had inferior status. Some Arabs believed that all Muslims should be treated equally. Over time, because most of the conquered peoples gradually converted to Islam, Arab and non-Arab Muslims began to intermingle.

A movement to promote Islamic spirituality arose under a preacher named Hasan al-Basri (642–728). He advocated a simple lifestyle and taught his followers to meditate (think deeply in silence) on the inner meaning of the Qur'an. This was the beginning of Sufism, a mystical movement within Islam. Although he disagreed with the luxurious lifestyle of the Umayyads, al-Basri did not oppose their rule. However, the Shia maintained that a member of Muhammad's family should reign. The leader of one Shia faction, Abu al-Abbas as-Saffah, claimed to be a descendant of the Prophet's uncle. Using this supposed family connection to muster support, he went on to defeat the Umayyads in 750 and proclaim the Abbasid dynasty.

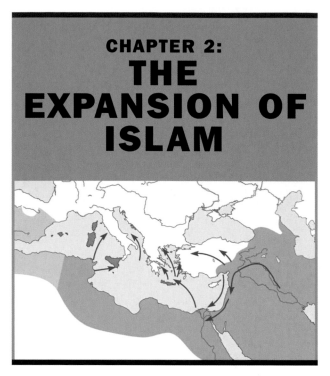

CHAPTER 2:
THE EXPANSION OF ISLAM

By 750, when the Abbasids came to power, the Islamic empire stretched from India to Spain. The Abbasids took power by claiming they were the rightful heirs of Muhammad. However, once in control, the Abbasid rulers began abandoning Muslim principles by living in luxury while most of their subjects remained in poverty. By the time of Caliph Harun ar-Rashid (reigned 764–809), the ruler lived in isolation from his subjects at the royal court in Baghdad (in present-day Iraq). The Shia along with other Muslim groups who hoped to return to the simpler society of the Prophet's time were unhappy about this development.

Abbasid advances Under the Abbasids, the Islamic empire became a major economic power. They encouraged the growth of industry and trade, and there were advances in technology, including the development of papermaking and irrigation (systems for watering crops). Harun ar-Rashid's reign is now also regarded as a golden age of cultural activity; the arts, Arabic grammar, literature, and music flourished. Centers of learning were established throughout the Muslim world, in Egypt, Morocco, Spain, Iran, and Mesopotamia (modern-day Iraq). The classical texts of the ancient Greek philosophers were translated from Greek and

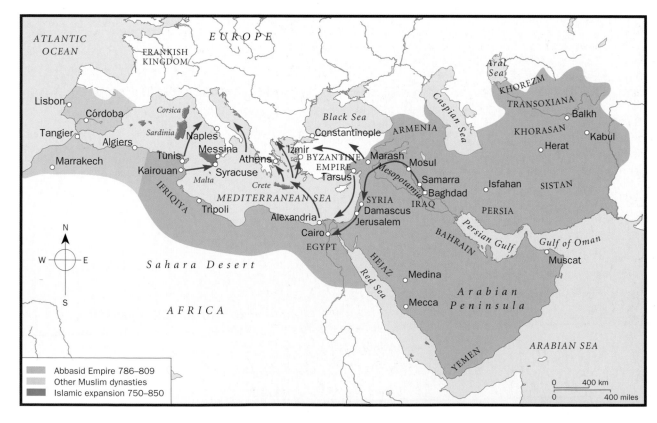

This map shows the Abbasid Empire in 850. By this time, there were several different Islamic dynasties.

Syriac into Arabic, enabling Muslim scholars to build on knowledge from the past. They made significant progress in science, mathematics, astronomy, and medicine. For example, Al-Khwarizmi (ca. 780–ca. 850) introduced Arabic numerals and the concept of algebra into European mathematics. The Iranian scholar Ibn-Sina (980–1037), also known as Avicenna, compiled the *Canon of Medicine*, a vast encyclopedia of medical knowledge.

SUFISM

Sufism, which began in the eighth century CE, is the mystical aspect of Islam. Sufis shun worldly wealth and seek an inner, spiritual life. They spend time in prayer and contemplation in order to become closer to God. From the twelfth century, the Sufi movement became organized through the establishment of Sufi orders, led by Sufi *pirs*, or leaders.

Sharia From the eighth century CE, a comprehensive Islamic code was developed, called the sharia (path to be followed). Sharia law was based on the Qur'an and the Sunna. During the ninth and tenth centuries, Muslim rulers encouraged leading scholars to write down the law. Five schools of law were named after the men who initiated them—four Sunni and one Shia. Sharia law contains rules for organizing society as well as rules for governing the behavior of individuals toward each other and in relation to God. Many rulers of Muslim territories developed an additional legal system that helped them in the day-to-day needs of government, especially to deal with matters of crime, property disputes, and commerce.

An illustration of Sufi mystics from Pakistan. The Sufis helped spread Islam throughout the world. They played an important role in educating people and reinforcing the spiritual aspect of the religion.

A divided empire

Although the Abbasid dynasty lasted until 1258, by the tenth century the Abbasid rulers were unable to command authority over all of the Muslim lands. In 945, the Buyids from Iran took control of the empire's capital, Baghdad, and ruled western Iran and Mesopotamia until 1055. The Abbasid caliph remained the symbolic head of the empire, but its regions were ruled by independent regimes, including the Caliphate of Córdoba in Spain and the Fatimid Empire in Egypt.

A portrait of Ibn-Rushd, also known as Averroës. Few translated works of Aristotle existed in Europe before he translated them into Latin and enabled scholars to study these important ancient texts once again.

IBN-RUSHD (1126–1198)

The writings of Spanish Muslim scholars had a significant influence in Europe. Among the most influential was Ibn-Rushd, who was trained in Islamic law, medicine, and philosophy. He became chief *qadi* (judge) of Córdoba. In the 1150s or 1160s, he was asked by the Almohad caliph to provide a correct interpretation of the Greek philosopher Aristotle. He presented Aristotle's thoughts clearly, helping readers understand them. Ibn-Rushd's work remained influential in Europe and the Islamic world for centuries after his death.

The Caliphate of Córdoba A Muslim army first entered Spain from North Africa in 711 and established an Islamic kingdom in the south and central Iberian Peninsula that became known as Al-Andalus. Muslim rule in Spain dramatically changed following the collapse of the Umayyads. When the Abbasids assumed power in Baghdad in 750, they massacred members of the Umayyad clan to secure control. One Umayyad prince, Abd ar-Rahman, escaped to Spain. In 756, he initiated a new Umayyad dynasty in Spain called the Caliphate of Córdoba.

By the tenth century, Córdoba, the capital of Al-Andalus, was one of the world's most advanced cities. It had clean, paved streets, running water, and 70 libraries. Córdoba's Great Mosque was an impressive architectural accomplishment. The Muslim rulers allowed Christians and Jews to practice their religion and to work and study freely, enabling an exchange of ideas and learning among Muslim, Jewish, and Christian scholars. Because of this, Córdoba became a major center of culture and learning.

Between the eleventh and thirteenth centuries, Al-Andalus was controlled by two Muslim dynasties from North Africa: the Almoravids (1056–1147) and the Almohads (1130–1269). During this period, the Christian rulers of northern Spain fought to regain control over the region. After centuries of struggle, the Christians achieved their goal, and Muslim rule ended in 1492.

The Fatimids The Shia caliphate of the Fatimids was established in Tunisia, North Africa, when Abdallah al-Mahdi took power. He claimed to be a descendant of Ali and his wife Fatima, a daughter of Muhammad. In 972, the Fatimids moved their capital to Cairo, Egypt. At its height in the mid-eleventh century, the Fatimid Empire ruled North Africa, Egypt, Syria, Palestine, and much of Arabia. It subsequently fell into decline, due to the growing power of the Seljuk Turks.

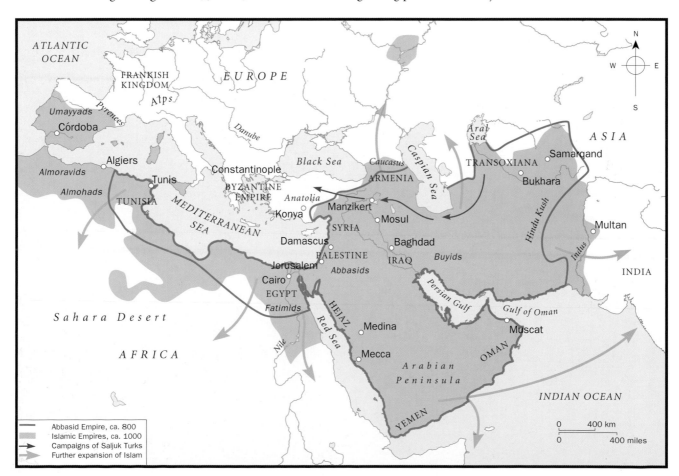

This map shows the various Islamic empires from around 800 CE to 1200 CE, as well as the further expansion of Islam.

13

The ruins of Qalaat al-Gindi, a fort built in the Sinai desert in Egypt by Saladin as protection against the crusaders and to guard the pilgrimage routes to Mecca.

The Seljuks In 1055, the Seljuk Turks—a dynasty that had converted to Islam in the 990s—seized power from the Buyids in Baghdad. The Abbasid caliph crowned their leader as sultan, the new title used by Muslim rulers. The Seljuks agreed to uphold Islamic law and defend Islam from its enemies. Each district of the Seljuk Empire—which included a large part of central Asia, Iran, Mesopotamia, Syria, and Palestine—was ruled by local military governors along with the Muslim clergy, the ulema, whose authority came from the Qur'an. Religious schools called madrassas were set up throughout the empire to provide formal training for the ulema. The ulema took charge of the legal system through the sharia courts, giving them considerable power in their local area.

The Crusades The Seljuks' commitment to defend Islam was soon put to the test. In 1071, they were attacked by an army of the Christian Byzantine Empire near Manzikert (in modern-day Turkey). Although they were victorious in this battle, by the end of the century, the Seljuk Empire was divided and weak. At this time of Muslim disunity, Pope Urban II, the head of the Roman Catholic Church, launched a series of military expeditions known as the Crusades to try to halt the spread of Islam and win back the Holy Land (Palestine).

In 1099, Christian crusaders from western Europe attacked Jerusalem. A sacred city for Christians, Muslims, and Jews, Jerusalem is the third holiest city in the Islamic world after Mecca and Medina. It is the site of the Dome of the Rock mosque that is built over a shrine that is sacred to Muslims and Jews. The crusaders succeeded in conquering Jerusalem and established Christian states in Palestine, Lebanon, and Anatolia (part of modern-day Turkey).

In 1171, a Kurdish general called Saladin overthrew the Fatimid dynasty in Egypt. Between 1174 and 1186, he united the Muslim territories of Syria, northern Mesopotamia, and Palestine under his leadership. He proceeded to lead a jihad, or struggle, against the crusaders. Saladin recaptured Jerusalem in 1187 and established his own dynasty, the Ayyubids.

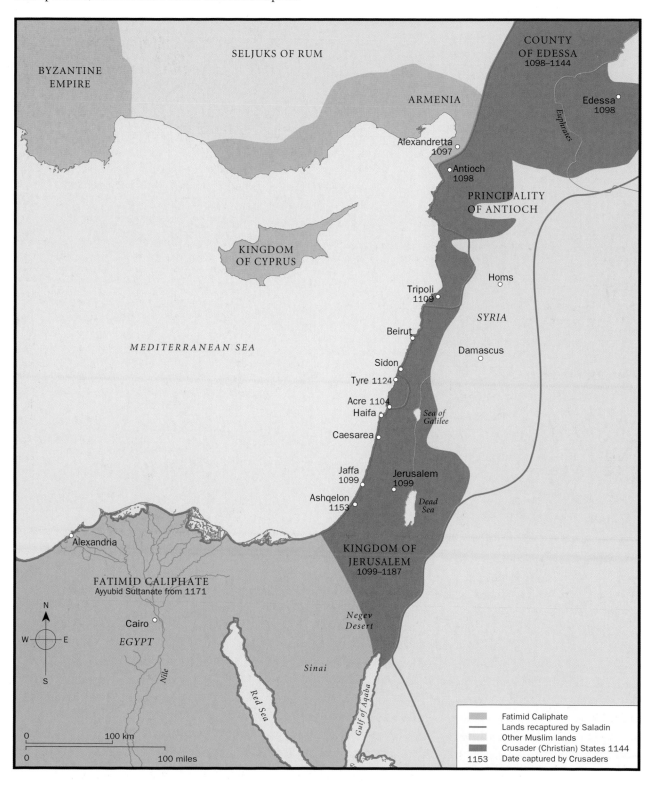

The Crusader States in 1144. Christian rule in the region was short-lived.

Further expansion Islam did not expand through war and conquest alone. Muslim traders helped spread Islam to distant regions, far from the Islamic heartlands, including East and West Africa, India, and many lands bordering the Indian Ocean.

Africa In the seventh century CE, Arab conquerors reached Aswan, Egypt and continued to move south into East Africa. The Funj dynasty in modern-day Sudan converted to Islam in the sixteenth century. The region was close to Arabia, so the Arab influence was strong. Arab and Iranian traders and settlers mixed with the local people, and a new culture developed from this interaction, which became known as Swahili. The Swahili language, for example, mixes the African language Bantu with Arabic words and is written using the Arabic alphabet.

In West Africa, the spread of Islam was mainly peaceful, and Islamic customs merged with local practices. Before 600 CE, trading posts had developed between the Maghreb (modern-day Morocco) and the Sahel (the area between the Sahara Desert and the tropical forests of Guinea). After the mid-600s, when

MANSA MUSA (1307–32)

The best-known West African Muslim ruler of the Middle Ages was the King of Mali, Mansa Musa (also known as Kankan Moussa.) After making the pilgrimage to Mecca in 1324–25, he built magnificent mosques, libraries, and madrassas throughout the Mali Empire to encourage Islamic learning. The Arab traveler Ibn Battuta admired the people of Mali for their learning of the Qur'an, noting how "they put their children in chains if they show any backwardness in memorizing it, and they are not set free until they know it by heart."

A mosque in Djenné, Mali. Under the Mali Empire, Djenné was a thriving town. Several examples of Islamic architecture from this era remain in the city today.

North Africa became part of the Islamic empire, the ideas of Islam spread south by traders. Many West African royal families converted voluntarily to the new religion, which they believed gave them prestige. They funded religious scholarship to further increase their status. Timbuktu, or Tombouctou, on the Niger River became the most impressive center of Islamic culture in Africa.

Indian Ocean

The Islamic empire also took control of the trade routes in the Indian Ocean. By 1500, Muslim traders influenced business in India, China, the Melaka Islands, and beyond. Muslim communities flourished. There is evidence of Muslim settlements on the islands of Pemba, Zanzibar, Mafia, and Kilwa between 1000 and 1150. The Arab traveler Ibn Battuta (ca. 1304–ca. 1377) established Muslim communities along the southern coastline of China.

India

Islam first appeared in India in 711 CE when the Arabs invaded Sind (in modern-day, southeastern Pakistan). The conquest of the Indian subcontinent began with the Ghurids, who occupied northern India in the late twelfth century. An independent sultanate was formed in Delhi that lasted from 1206 to 1526. Some of the early Muslim rulers destroyed Hindu temples and replaced them with large mosques to show their dominance. However, under the Tughluq dynasty (1320–1413), a tolerant religious policy was established. By the mid-1300s, the Delhi Sultanate covered all of India except for the southern tip and the west coast. Possibly 20 to 25 percent of the population of the Delhi Sultanate converted to Islam, while the rest remained Hindu. Those who did convert to Islam combined Islamic practices with local Hindu rituals, since Hinduism is a religion that willingly incorporates other religious practices.

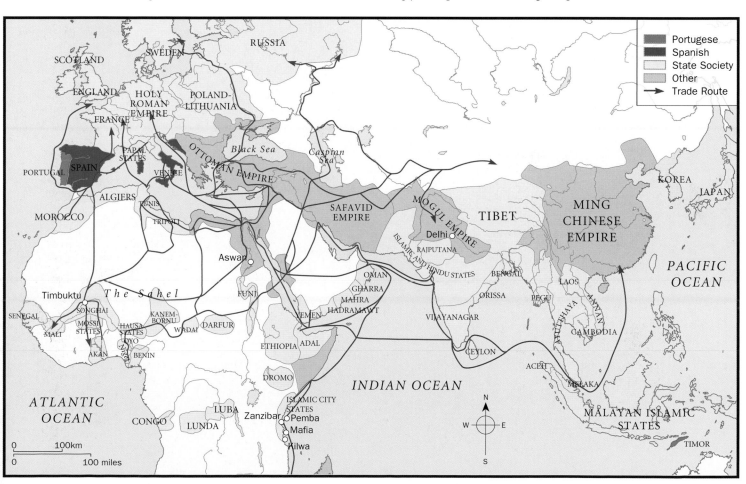

This map shows world trade routes and empires around 1500. By the end of the fifteenth century, Islam had reached eastern Europe, the plains of central Asia, and large parts of Africa. It had spread to northern India, China, and the Malayan states.

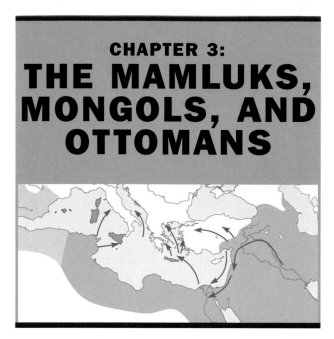

CHAPTER 3:
THE MAMLUKS, MONGOLS, AND OTTOMANS

Mamluks Beginning around 900 CE, it was common for Muslim rulers to buy slaves to fight as warriors in their armies. These warrior-slaves were known as mamluks. Once freed, some mamluks rose in society, and a few even became rulers. It was the mamluk soldiers who put an end to Saladin's Ayyubid dynasty in 1250. They proclaimed their own sultan and initiated a period of rule that lasted until about 1500. Based in Cairo, the Mamluks demonstrated their devotion to Islam by funding the Sufi orders and Islamic scholarship and constructing elaborate mosques. By 1517, the Mamluks were defeated by the Ottomans.

Mongols Meanwhile, in Mongolia, a new empire was developing. Established in the thirteenth century by the ruthless leader Genghis Khan (ca. 1162–1227), the Mongol Empire stretched from northern China in the east to modern-day Germany in the west. After Genghis Khan's death, his descendants created several separate Mongol states that sometimes fought each other as well as outside peoples. In their early conquests, the Mongols

From the thirteenth to fifteenth centuries, the Islamic empires of the Mamluks and Mongols rose and fell. The end of the period witnessed the rise of the Ottoman Empire that survived for 500 years.

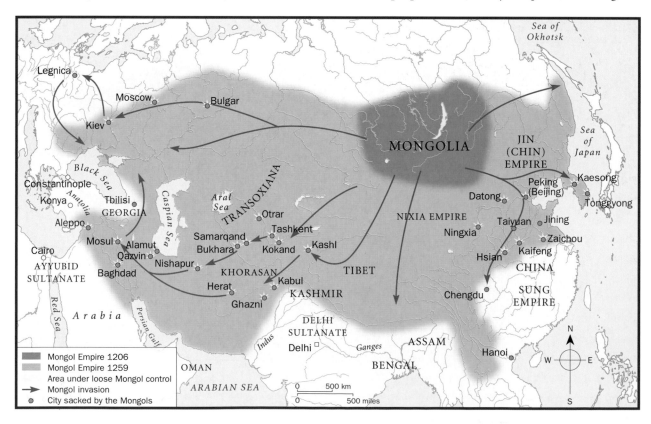

The Mongol invasions of the thirteenth century. The Mongols' knowledge of the latest warfare techniques enabled them to wreak destruction on a huge scale.

Whirling Dervishes in the dance hall in Rumi's adopted hometown of Konya, Turkey, where he died. The mosque, dance hall, and tombs of leaders of his Sufi order still attract pilgrims today.

unleashed massive destruction on their enemies. They massacred entire populations of cities and destroyed all of the buildings. In 1258, the Mongols defeated the Abbasid caliphate and toppled Baghdad. It took them 40 days to execute all the inhabitants of the city.

However, in the following years, the leader of one of the Mongol states named Hülegü converted to Islam. By the beginning of the fourteenth century, all of the western Mongol states had followed his example. The Mongols began to rebuild the cities they had destroyed and became patrons of the arts, sciences, mathematics, and history.

RUMI (1207–73)

The Sufi mystic and poet Jalal ad-Din ar-Rumi lived through the destruction of the Mongol invasions. In about 1218, with the Mongols approaching, Rumi and his family escaped their native city of Khorasan in eastern Iran and made their way to Konya in Anatolia. Rumi's experience led him to initiate a mystical movement that helped people come to terms with the disaster. After his death, his followers formed a Sufi order often called the Whirling Dervishes. They performed a spinning dance so they could enter a trance and become one with God. Rumi wrote about 30,000 verses and many Rubaiyat stanzas, a form of Iranian poetry. This is one of them:

> As salt resolved in the ocean
> I was swallowed in God's sea,
> Past faith, past unbelieving,
> Past doubt, past certainty.
>
> Suddenly in my bosom
> A star shone clear and bright;
> All the suns of heaven
> Vanished in that star's light.

The Robaiyat of Jalal ad-Din ar-Rumi: Select Translations into English Verse by A. J. Arberry, 1949

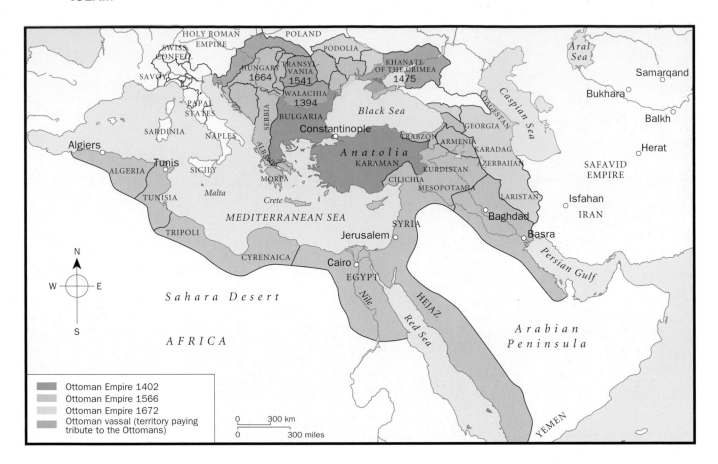

The rise of the Ottoman Empire (1328–1672). It became the most expansive of the Islamic empires.

By the mid-fourteenth century, the Mongol states were in decline. The Mongol general Timur (ca. 1336–1405), also known as Tamerlane, attempted to reverse this change in fortunes. He conquered much of central Asia, Mesopotamia, and Iran, as well as the cities of Delhi, India, and Ankara in modern-day Turkey. Under Timur and his successors, Herat, Samarqand, and Bukhara (all in central Asia) became splendid cities. Timur made Samarqand his capital. He brought craftspeople from all over the empire to construct the city. He also invited scholars, artists, and historians to settle in Samarqand and develop it as a center of Islamic culture. Although he was Sunni, he protected Shias in his empire.

The Ottomans
As the Mongol states were declining, the Ottomans, a Turkish tribe, were establishing an empire in Anatolia. By 1400, the Ottomans had conquered Serbia, Bulgaria, and most of the Byzantine Empire. In 1453, the Ottoman ruler Sultan Mehmet II took the Byzantine city of Constantinople and

renamed it Istanbul. The empire continued to expand. By the mid-1500s, the Ottomans had captured most of Hungary and controlled a vast area of Europe, stretching from the Crimea to southern Greece. They also conquered a large area of the Islamic lands during the sixteenth century, including eastern Anatolia, northern Mesopotamia, Syria, Yemen, and North Africa (from Egypt to Algeria).

The Ottoman Empire was able to expand largely because of its effective army. Like other Muslim rulers, the Ottomans used slave soldiers. Their elite troops were the Janissaries. Taken from Christian families as boys, they were converted to Islam and trained as soldiers. Because they were outsiders and completely dependent on the sultan for their position, the Janissaries were fiercely loyal to their ruler.

The Ottomans maintained a firm grip on their empire. It was divided into provinces, each ruled by a pasha, or general, who was directly responsible to the sultan. The sultan appointed qadis to run the justice

The Mosque of Süleyman in Istanbul was the largest mosque ever built in the Ottoman Empire. Sinan adapted the Hagia Sophia church design to include large open spaces where Muslims could pray together.

system based on sharia law, which became the official law for all Muslims. The Ottomans brought the ulema under their control. The ulema provided religious leadership and helped the people accept Ottoman rule.

There were many different religious and ethnic groups living within the empire, including Christians, Arabs, Jews, Berbers (native North Africans), and Turks. Although the sultan exerted strong religious control over Muslims through sharia law, he allowed other communities to follow their own customs, and it was possible for non-Muslims to achieve high rank within the empire. However, the Ottomans had a different attitude toward the peoples outside their empire. They saw themselves as defenders of Islam against the religion's enemies. As Sunni Muslims, not only did they fight the Christians to the west, they also fought the Shia Safavids to the east.

THE MOSQUE OF SÜLEYMAN

Under Sultan Süleyman, Ottoman culture reached its height. He patronized art, history, medicine, and architecture. One of his crowning achievements was the Mosque of Süleyman in Istanbul, constructed to rival the 1,000-year-old Hagia Sophia church. The architect, Sinan, based the general layout of the mosque on the design of Hagia Sophia. The mosque was built in the 1550s and had four minaret towers. Within the complex there was a madrassa, a hospital, a dining hall, a caravansary (inn for travelers), baths, hospices, and shops.

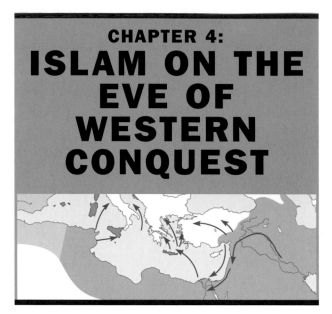

CHAPTER 4:
ISLAM ON THE EVE OF WESTERN CONQUEST

The Safavids In 1501, the founder of the Safavid Empire, Shah Ismail, conquered Tabriz (in present-day Iran). Over the next 10 years, he conquered the rest of Iran and the Iraqi provinces of Baghdad and Mosul. Shah Ismail declared Shia Islam to be the religion of his empire, although most of the population was Sunni. The Shia nature of the empire brought it into conflict with the Sunni Ottomans. In 1514, the Ottoman ruler Selim I (1467–1520) defeated the Safavids at the Battle of Chaldiran and went on to gain control of eastern Anatolia.

However, later that century, the Safavid ruler Shah Abbas I (1571–1629) achieved significant victories against the Ottomans. Within his empire, he strengthened Shia Islam by bringing in Shia ulema from other countries and building Shia madrassas. He introduced annual rituals to mourn the death of the Prophet's grandson Hussain at Karbala. A procession of mourners expressed an emotional outpouring of grief, as if Hussain had recently been killed. Grieving for Hussain became central to religious life, and Shia Islam became an important part of Iran's national identity.

During the sixteenth and seventeenth centuries, Islamic empires controlled large territories in eastern Europe, western Asia, and India, as well as the Middle East and North Africa. These empires, known as the Safavids, Moguls, and Ottomans, all gradually weakened, but Islam continued to expand outside the core Muslim regions.

Under Shah Abbas's reign, the capital, Isfahan (also called Esfahan), became a cultural center. The art of Iranian miniatures flourished, and the city was filled with elaborate palaces and parks, along with great mosques and madrassas. Yet by the late seventeenth century, the empire was in decline. After Nadir Shah was assassinated in 1747, the central government collapsed in Iran. There was a period of anarchy (a state of lawlessness), with the Ottomans and Russians controlling the north and various tribal chiefs competing for power in the south. However, the ulema retained the loyalty and

The courtyard and pool of the Imam Mosque in Isfahan, Iran.

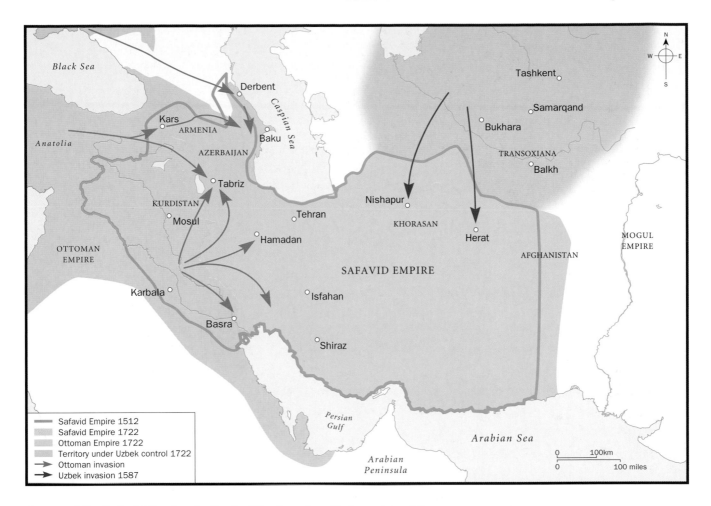

A map of the Safavid Empire, indicating the invasions that weakened it.

religious devotion of the Iranian people. When a new dynasty, the Qajars, seized control of Iran in 1779, the ulema retained their important position.

The Moguls The Mogul emperors in India were Sunni Muslims. In 1526, the first Mogul emperor, Babur (1483–1530), conquered Delhi and paved the way for the conquest of northern India. His grandson, Akbar (1556–1605), extended Mogul power over most of the country. He was a tolerant ruler, respectful of all faiths. Akbar abolished the tax charged to non-Muslims that had been imposed by Muslim rulers in all their conquered territories since the seventh century. He became a vegetarian and gave up hunting so that he would not offend the Hindus, who believe in treating animals well. Akbar built Hindu temples and established a house of worship where scholars of all religions could meet and hold discussions.

MUSLIM SHRINES

Shrines with images of saints have always played an important role in Indian Islam. This contrasts with other Muslim areas where the use of images in worship is discouraged. Shrines dedicated to the memory of the great Sufi saints were established at their tombs. The shrines were seen as a gateway to God and attendants would carry out daily rituals there, such as washing and decorating it. One example of these shrines is the tomb of the Muslim saint Khawaja Moinuddin Chishti, which includes a magnificent mosque built by the Mogul emperor Shah Jahan (ruled 1628–58). For the Muslims of India, it is considered the next most important holy place after Mecca and Medina.

The Sufi orders helped spread Islam in India. The Sufi *pirs* inspired the conversions of tribal peoples and the lower Hindu castes—people who were disadvantaged under the Hindu social system. The pirs used local languages to teach the message of Islam.

Akbar's grandson, Shah Jahan, continued to extend Mogul power. Known for the splendor of his court and his passion for building, Shah Jahan ordered the building of the Taj Mahal, a monument in memory of his wife, Mumtaz Mahal. He also built a huge palace in Delhi called the Red Fort and the Jama Masjid in Agra, one of the most spectacular mosques in the country.

Shah Jahan was relatively tolerant toward his Hindu subjects, but his son, Shah Aurangzeb (ruled 1658–1707), also know as Alamgir, ordered the destruction of many Hindu temples, reintroduced the tax payable by non-Muslims, and stopped Shia Muslims from holding celebrations in memory of Hussain. He forbade the drinking of wine and banned music at court. These policies reflected the growing reformist movement.

Aurangzeb's religious policies provoked major revolts against the regime, and the Mogul Empire began to weaken. Hindu and Sikh rulers conquered parts of northern India. In 1739, the Iranian ruler Nadir Shah invaded northern India and sacked Delhi. The British, who had entered India as traders, took advantage of Mogul decline and began to take control of the Indian states. Indian Muslims realized they were losing power.

WALI ALLAH AND THE REFORMIST MOVEMENT

Wali Allah (ca. 1702–62) grew up during the Mogul Empire decline. He became one of the leaders of a reformist movement in Islam. Wali Allah believed that to revive Islamic power, Indian Muslims should be unified among themselves and strengthen relations with the rest of the Muslim world. They should not merge their customs with other Indian traditions. Muslims should return to a more traditional form of Islamic practice, stripped of Indian adaptations such as the worship of saints. The reformist message was attractive to educated Muslims, but it had less impact among the much larger numbers of poorer Muslims who continued to worship at shrines and enjoy lively popular festivals.

Ottoman weakness The Ottoman Empire also began to decline in the later seventeenth century, when European countries grew more powerful at its expense. Like the other Islamic empires, the economy of the Ottoman Empire was based largely on agriculture and long-established trading relationships. It lacked the

The well known monument in India—the Taj Mahal.

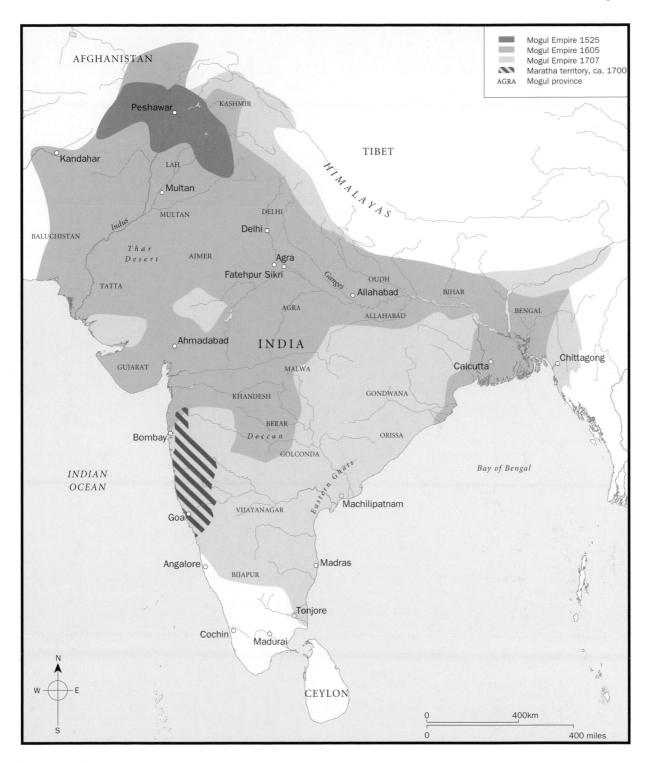

A map illustrating the expansion of the Mogul Empire throughout much of India between 1526 and 1707.

opportunity for further expansion. By contrast, the economies of Europe's major powers grew rapidly from the seventeenth to the nineteenth centuries due to the trade with the Americas and East Asia and the expanding technological advances that led to large-scale industrialization. In the late seventeenth and eighteenth centuries, the Ottomans lost territory to European powers, including the Habsburgs, the Venetians, the Poles, and the Russians. The empire gradually broke up and eventually collapsed in the early 1920s.

Islam around the world

While the empires of the Safavids, the Moguls, and the Ottomans crumbled, Islam flourished in other parts of the world. Around 1500, Islam came to Southeast Asia, arising peacefully through trade rather than conquest. Around 1524, the first major Muslim state in this region was established in Aceh in northern Sumatra. Makassar and Mataram became Muslim states in the early seventeenth century. As in India, Sufi teachers presented Islamic teachings in a way that Hindus could understand. Islamic customs often intermingled with the local traditions of Hinduism and animism, which is the belief that spirits of nature and people's ancestors could influence fortunes in the present. The extension of Islam continued despite conquests in the region by Portugal and the Netherlands—both Christian powers.

West Africa

In the eighteenth and nineteenth centuries, a series of jihad movements in West Africa led to the establishment of a number of Islamic states. The leaders of these movements were generally ulema who had studied with Sufi masters and preached a reformist version of Islam. The most famous jihad leader was Usman Dan Fodio who set up the Sokoto Caliphate in the early nineteenth century.

The movements were supported by other people who did not fit into society, such as runaway slaves. They were also supported by cattle herders of the Fulani tribe—from present-day Nigeria and other West African countries—who were unhappy about the taxes imposed by local kings. One Fulani scholar fought local rulers and, in 1725, set up an Islamic state called Futa Jallon, or Fouta Djallon, in modern-day Guinea.

Sir Siddiq Abubakar III, a former sultan of Sokoto, who ruled the Sokoto Caliphate from 1938 to 1988. After the British brought Sokoto under their control in 1903, the role became increasingly ceremonial, although the sultan still has influence over the Fulani and Hausa peoples of northern Nigeria.

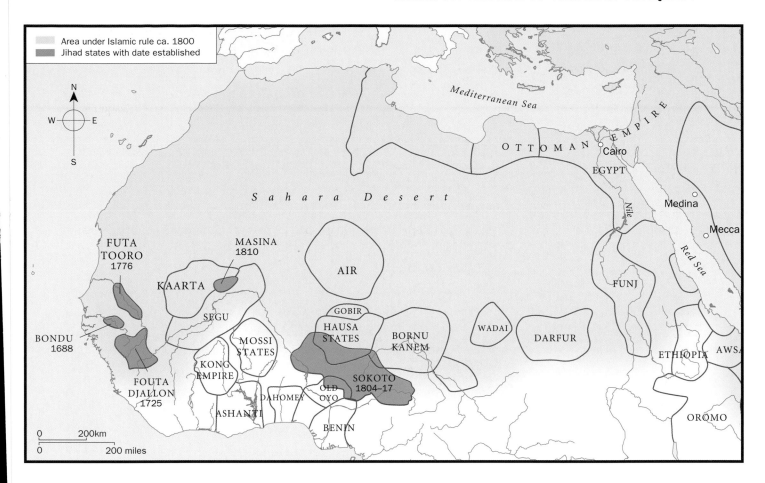

Area under Islamic rule ca. 1800
Jihad states with date established

This map depicts the jihad states in about 1800 and indicates the extent of Islam in West Africa at the time.

Russia In the fifteenth century, the Christian kingdom of Russia began to take over lands in Central Asia that were inhabited by large numbers of Muslims. Despite the shift to Christian rule, there was no decline in the popularity of Islam in this region, and there are still large numbers of Muslims in Central Asia today.

USMAN DAN FODIO (1754–1817)

A Muslim scholar and teacher, Usman Dan Fodio came from the Hausa kingdom of Gobir (northwestern Nigeria). During the 1780s and 1790s, his reputation as a religious and political leader grew. He gained support from the Hausa peasants, who believed he was the Mahdi, the twelfth Imam in Shia tradition who would return to the world to restore justice. In 1802, a conflict arose between Dan Fodio's community and the rulers of Gobir, so Dan Fodio made a migration 30 miles (48 km) north to Gudu and became the imam (leader of the Muslim community) there. He set up a caliphate based on the simple social justice of the Prophet's community in Medina.

Soon after, Dan Fodio raised an army and launched a jihad against the Hausa rulers. By 1808, he had overthrown most of the Hausa kingdoms to form the Sokoto Caliphate. It expanded over the following two decades to include most of present-day northern Nigeria and the northern Cameroons. After the success of the jihad, Dan Fodio retired from public life. He grew concerned that the new rulers had become as unjust as the old ones and that his reforming ideals had been forgotten.

In the early twentieth century, a new generation of Muslim reformers arose, led by the Egyptian Hasan al-Banna (1906–49). In 1928, al-Banna established the Muslim Brotherhood, an Islamic movement for social justice. Al-Banna had witnessed British colonists living in luxury, while Egyptian workers lived in poverty. To him, this was a religious problem, and the solution was an Islamic government, in control of the religious, economic, social, and cultural life of the country. Al-Banna believed that Muslims needed to make a jihad to reform society. The Qur'an should be interpreted to meet the requirements of modern society, which included the struggle for social justice.

Not only did the Brotherhood train followers in Muslim beliefs, but they also built clinics and hospitals and set up factories where workers received fair pay. A majority of the members accepted that social welfare was a vital part of spreading the Islamic way of life;

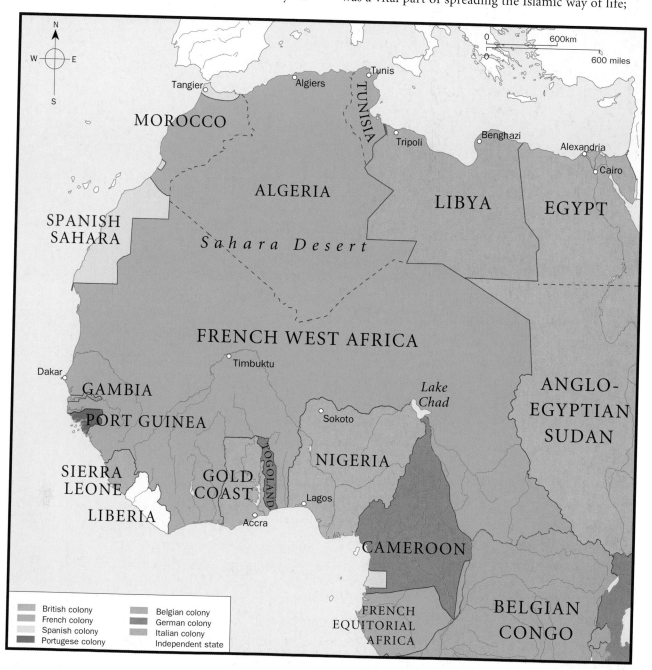

Northwest Africa in 1914. The French dominated the region, and only two countries were free of colonial control.

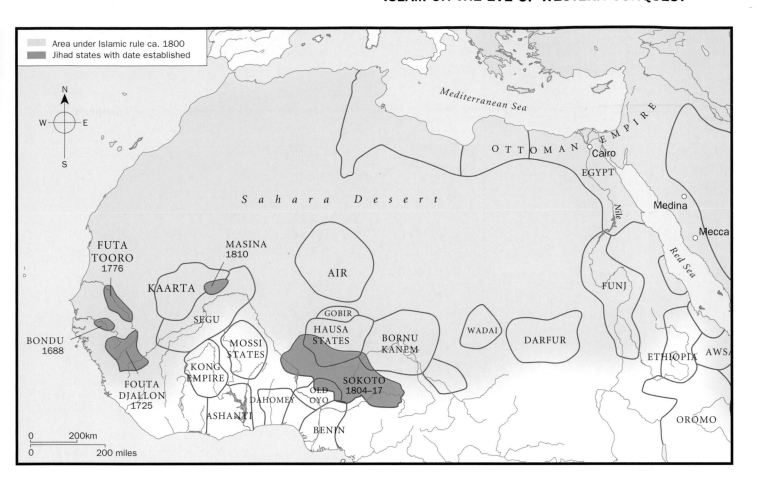

This map depicts the jihad states in about 1800 and indicates the extent of Islam in West Africa at the time.

Russia In the fifteenth century, the Christian kingdom of Russia began to take over lands in Central Asia that were inhabited by large numbers of Muslims. Despite the shift to Christian rule, there was no decline in the popularity of Islam in this region, and there are still large numbers of Muslims in Central Asia today.

USMAN DAN FODIO (1754–1817)

A Muslim scholar and teacher, Usman Dan Fodio came from the Hausa kingdom of Gobir (northwestern Nigeria). During the 1780s and 1790s, his reputation as a religious and political leader grew. He gained support from the Hausa peasants, who believed he was the Mahdi, the twelfth Imam in Shia tradition who would return to the world to restore justice. In 1802, a conflict arose between Dan Fodio's community and the rulers of Gobir, so Dan Fodio made a migration 30 miles (48 km) north to Gudu and became the imam (leader of the Muslim community) there. He set up a caliphate based on the simple social justice of the Prophet's community in Medina.

Soon after, Dan Fodio raised an army and launched a jihad against the Hausa rulers. By 1808, he had overthrown most of the Hausa kingdoms to form the Sokoto Caliphate. It expanded over the following two decades to include most of present-day northern Nigeria and the northern Cameroons. After the success of the jihad, Dan Fodio retired from public life. He grew concerned that the new rulers had become as unjust as the old ones and that his reforming ideals had been forgotten.

CHAPTER 5:
ISLAM UNDER COLONIAL RULE

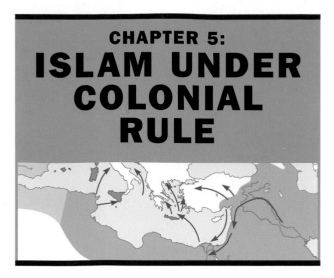

The rapid expansion of the European economies beginning in the eighteenth century had a disastrous impact on the Islamic world. European countries needed new markets, so they conquered large areas of the Muslim world in North Africa, the Middle East, and Asia. They created colonies there to draw the Muslims into their trade network. The new European rulers ran the colonies in their own interests. They bought large quantities of food and raw materials, such as sugar, tea, cotton, and wool, from the colonies. They also sold cheap, manufactured goods to the colonies, which caused the failure of the colonies' own industries. For example, British exports of cotton goods to India destroyed the local cotton industry. As a result, Islamic countries became economically dependent on the West.

By 1922, after the defeat of the Ottoman Empire, the majority of Muslim society was under colonial rule. Britain ruled Egypt, Palestine, India, Sudan, Aden, Oman, Kuwait, Qatar, Tanganyika, and the Malay states. France controlled northwestern Africa, Lebanon, and Syria.

India There were frequent challenges to colonial rule. In India, the most famous challenge to the British was the Indian Revolt of 1857. Bengali Muslim soldiers in the British Army erupted in mutiny upon discovering that the army used beef and pork fat to grease the rifle cartridges. This practice was offensive to Hindus, who consider cows to be sacred, and to Muslims, for whom pigs are unclean. As well as expressing their anger at colonial policies that were draining the country of its natural resources, Muslims feared that their faith and culture were under attack.

In order to disunite the opposition to their rule and make their position more secure, the British encouraged divisions between Hindus and Muslims. For instance, in 1909, the Indian Councils Act set up separate Hindu and

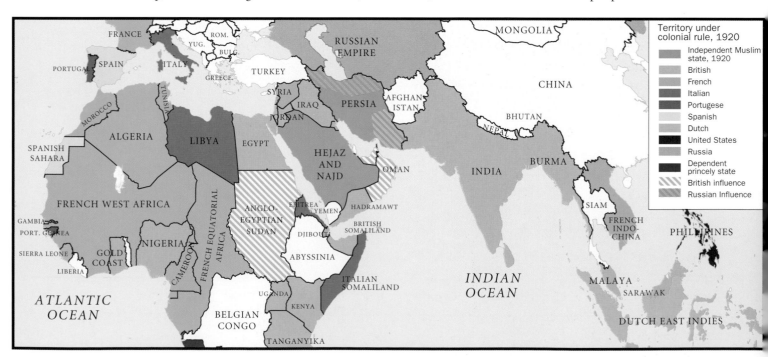

The extent of European control over Muslim countries in 1920.

A contemporary European illustration portraying Indians fighting British soldiers during the mutiny in Lucknow, northern India, in July 1957.

Muslim electorates at the local level. Electorates are groups of people who have the right to vote, so this created a separate legal and political identity for the Hindus and the Muslims. Actions like these helped promote the idea that the two religions formed separate nations within India.

Egypt From 1882, Britain controlled Egypt. The British took over Egypt's cotton production and built ports, railways, and the Suez Canal to help them to transport goods and manage the economy. Taxes for local people were greatly increased to fund these massive projects, even though Europeans living in Egypt paid very little tax. There was widespread resistance to this policy and other aspects of colonial rule. The Islamic reform movements became involved in this resistance. Influential reformers Muhammad Abduh (1849–1905) and Jamal al-Din al-Afghani (1838–97) initiated the Salafiyyah movement. As a response to European domination, they promoted the idea of Pan-Islamism—Muslim unity across national boundaries.

THE SALAFIYYAH MOVEMENT

To achieve Muslim unity and restore the spiritual strength of Islam, Muhammad Abduh believed that Muslims should return to the principles of social justice practiced by the early Muslim community. But he believed that these principles should be adjusted to fit with modern democratic values. All sources of Muslim law, including the Qur'an and the Sunna, should be open to debate by all Muslims. It should be possible to change an Islamic law in accordance with modern requirements. Muhammad Abduh stated, "If a ruling has become the cause of harm which it did not cause before, then we must change it according to the prevailing [current] conditions."

ISLAM

In the early twentieth century, a new generation of Muslim reformers arose, led by the Egyptian Hasan al-Banna (1906–49). In 1928, al-Banna established the Muslim Brotherhood, an Islamic movement for social justice. Al-Banna had witnessed British colonists living in luxury, while Egyptian workers lived in poverty. To him, this was a religious problem, and the solution was an Islamic government, in control of the religious, economic, social, and cultural life of the country. Al-

Banna believed that Muslims needed to make a jihad to reform society. The Qur'an should be interpreted to meet the requirements of modern society, which included the struggle for social justice.

Not only did the Brotherhood train followers in Muslim beliefs, but they also built clinics and hospitals and set up factories where workers received fair pay. A majority of the members accepted that social welfare was a vital part of spreading the Islamic way of life;

Northwest Africa in 1914. The French dominated the region, and only two countries were free of colonial control.

Algerian boys cleaning the boots of French soldiers in 1960. In 1956, France had granted independence to Morocco and Tunisia, but Algerians were still waging a struggle for freedom from colonial rule.

a minority attempted to achieve their goals through terrorism. The ideas of the Muslim Brotherhood spread throughout the Middle East.

Muslims under French rule
French colonialism differed from British colonialism because French people were encouraged to settle in their country's colonies. After the French conquered Algeria, Morocco, and Tunisia in the nineteenth century, they handed over land to French and other European settlers.

By 1940, settlers occupied 35 to 40 percent of farmland in Algeria. The French also had a policy of assimilation—they wanted their subjects to adopt their culture. Under French rule, Muslim culture was suppressed. Traditional Islamic colleges were abolished or had their money taken away. In the 1920s and 1930s, Islamic reformers in Algeria joined nationalists to fight for independence from France, which they eventually won in 1962.

Hasan al-Banna explained the mission of the Muslim Brotherhood in a document entitled "Between Yesterday and Today":

Following these two aims [to free Egypt from foreign domination and to create a free Islamic state], we have some special aims without the realization of which our society cannot become completely Islamic. Brethren [brothers], recall that more than 60 percent of the Egyptians live at a subhuman level, that they get enough to eat only through the most arduous toil, and Egypt is threatened by murderous famines and exposed to many economic problems of which only Allah can know the outcome. Recall, too, that there are more than 320 foreign companies in Egypt, monopolizing [controlling] all public utilities and all important facilities in every part of the country. . . Among your aims are to work for the reform of education; to war against poverty, ignorance, disease, and crime; and to create an exemplary society which will deserve to be associated with the Islamic Sacred Law.

Nearly one million pilgrims face the Kaaba during sunset prayers at the Great Mosque in Mecca.

The Kingdom of Saudi Arabia

Unlike many other Muslim countries, Arabia was not colonized. In the mid-eighteenth century, an Arabian prince named Muhammad Ibn Saud made an alliance with Muhammad Ibn Abd al-Wahhab, an extreme Muslim reformer. After conquering Mecca and Medina, they set fire to all books except the Qur'an. They banned music and flowers and the use of tobacco and coffee from the holy cities. Men were forced to grow beards. Women had to be veiled and remain separate from men.

The Hajj

The hajj, or pilgrimage to Mecca, has been performed in Arabia since ancient times. Since Muhammad's time, pilgrimage rituals have been linked to events in his life, as well as to earlier deeds that are related in the Bible. The purpose of the hajj is to stop all worldly activities for a short time and focus on God alone. Pilgrims circle the Kaaba in Mecca seven times and kiss the Black Stone in the wall of the Kaaba. Then, they run seven times between the hills of Safa and Marwah in memory of Hagar's search for water for her child Ishmael, the forefather of the Arabs. They visit the plain of Arafat where Muhammad preached his final sermon. At Mina, they throw stones at three pillars that represent the devil. On the final day, they hold a feast to remember how the Prophet Abraham was willing to sacrifice his son for God.

Al-Wahhab's religious ideas later became known in the West as Wahhabism and Islamic fundamentalism.

In the early 1900s, one of Ibn Saud's descendants conquered the entire area of Arabia. In 1932, he proclaimed the foundation of the Kingdom of Saudi Arabia and became King Abd al-Aziz Ibn Saud. The Saudis claimed to be the heirs of pure Islam. They declared they would rule in the same way as the Muslims of the seventh century CE, following the Qur'an. Medieval punishments, such as cutting off the hand of a thief, became part of Saudi law. Yet some laws, such as the banning of alcohol and gambling, did not even exist in the Prophet's time.

Most Muslim organizations disagreed with this interpretation of Islam. For example, the Muslim Brotherhood criticized the use of Islamic punishments. They also claimed it was against Quranic values for Saudi Arabia's rulers to live in great luxury while most of the population lived in poverty. Nevertheless, Saudi Arabia remained significant to Muslims worldwide as the birthplace of Islam and their spiritual home. Pilgrims came in large numbers to visit the sacred sites to fulfill the hajj, the fifth pillar of Islam.

Another point of conflict among Muslims has been the strong connection between Saudi Arabia and Western countries, particularly the United States. In the 1930s, oil was discovered in the kingdom and an American company called the Arabian Oil Company (Aramco) helped the country extract its oil. Control of the oil industry made the U.S. the most influential foreign nation in Saudi Arabia. Many Muslims felt that an Islamic country should not have such close ties with the West.

Arabia in the 1920s. In the early twentieth century, Abd al-Aziz conquered the territory of Arabia and formed the kingdom of Saudi Arabia.

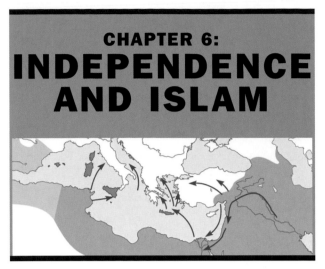

CHAPTER 6: INDEPENDENCE AND ISLAM

Most colonies with large Muslim populations gained their independence from European rule after World War II (1939–45). In some cases, such as India and Palestine, decolonization, or the process of gaining independence, increased the divisions between religious groups, leading to bloodshed. Some Muslim countries, such as Egypt, tried to separate religion from the government to form modern national states inspired by the West. But the failure of these national governments to sufficiently raise their people's living standards led many to oppose their rulers. Some became supporters of Communism, a system in which the state controls all the factories and agriculture. Communism was

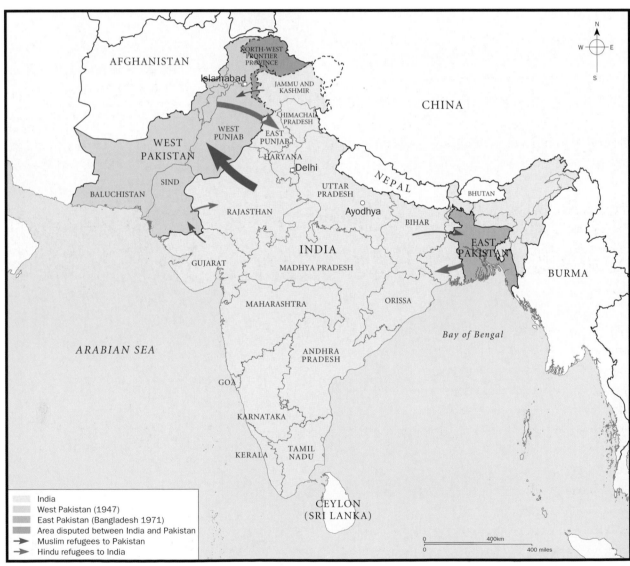

This map shows the partition of India in 1947 and subsequent movement of refugees; Pakistan was itself divided into Pakistan and Bangladesh in 1971.

EXTREMISM IN INDIA

Extremist Hindu organizations, such as the Bharatiya Janata Party (BJP), want to end secular (nonreligious) rule in India and establish Hinduism as the country's religion. In 1992, militant Hindus stormed the Ayodhya mosque in northern India and destroyed it, shouting "Hindustan [the Indian subcontinent] is for the Hindus" and "Death to Muslims." The demolition sparked some of the worst violence between Hindus and Muslims since partition. In a cycle of revenge attacks, Muslims attacked temples, and Hindus ransacked mosques. Around 2,000 people lost their lives in the riots.

In the 2000s, extreme Islamic groups in some places have carried out attacks on Hindus. For instance, in 2002, a group of Muslims attacked a train carrying religious Hindus. However, the extremists on both sides are a minority in India.

The tensions between India and Pakistan continue to the present day. The two countries are in dispute over the territory of Kashmir, which became divided during partition. India and Pakistan fought two wars over Kashmir, in 1947–48 and 1965. A further war in 1971 resulted in East Pakistan becoming a separate nation, Bangladesh. Some pro-Pakistan movements have sought the merging of Kashmir with Pakistan, while Kashmiri nationalist organizations have struggled for independence from both India and Pakistan. These movements have all been resisted by Indian forces.

In 1992, the residents of Ayodhya sift through the rubble of their town's mosque after it was destroyed by Hindu extremists.

practiced in the Soviet Union (formerly the Russian Empire) and had enabled an underdeveloped country to become a modern industrial state. Others looked to their faith for a solution, and a small minority joined radical Islamic movements.

India In 1947, India gained its independence from Britain. The country was divided in two. India became mainly Hindu, while the new state of Pakistan—split into East Pakistan and West Pakistan—was mostly Muslim. As soon as the new borders of the countries were known, around 10 million people fled their homes to the country where they hoped to be safe. Muslims in India rushed to Pakistan while Hindus and Sikhs fled in the opposite direction. Most Sikhs settled in Punjab in India, but they did not get their own state. During the exodus, one million people were murdered in ferocious religious massacres. The division between Muslim and Hindu was not merely based on religion—the groups were also divided under British colonial rule.

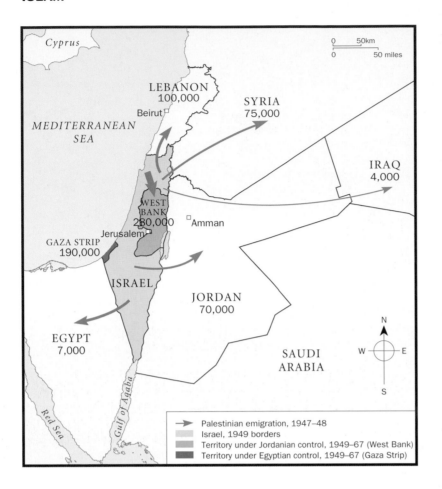

This map shows the dispersal of Palestinians to neighboring lands during the conflict of 1947–48. The majority remain refugees to this day.

HOLY SITES IN JERUSALEM

The city of Jerusalem, which has been under full Israeli control since the Arab-Israeli war of 1967, contains sites that are considered holy to Judaism, Islam, and Christianity. The most significant Jewish site is the Western Wall of the Temple Mount, regarded as the only remaining part of the Second Jewish Temple, which was destroyed in 70 CE. The Temple Mount, known in Arabic as Haram al-Sharif, also has two major Muslim shrines—the Dome of the Rock and the Al-Aqsa Mosque. For Christians, the Church of the Holy Sepulcher marks the place where Jesus was killed and has been an important pilgrimage destination since the fourth century CE.

The Arab-Israeli conflict As in India, the roots of the conflict between the mostly Muslim Arabs and the Jewish Israelis lie in colonial times. In the late nineteenth century, the Jewish people in eastern Europe were the target of persecution. They were blamed for the problems in society.

A minority of Jewish people believed that they could be safe only in their own state. Known as Zionists, they campaigned to make Palestine—the ancient home of the Jews—into a Jewish state. Jews started to emigrate to Palestine, which was under Ottoman rule until the British took control in 1918. Jewish emigration to Palestine increased during the 1920s and 1930s as anti-Semitism grew in Europe, culminating in the rise to power of the German,

June 1948: These Palestinians have left their village near Haifa, part of the new state of Israel, and are heading for Tulkarm in the West Bank. The Palestinians hoped they would be able to return to their homes some day.

anti-Semitic Nazi Party in 1933. The great majority of the inhabitants of Palestine were Arabs, who resented this large influx, and conflict arose between the Palestinian Arabs and the Jewish settlers.

By 1947, Britain was no longer able to control the growing conflict in Palestine, and asked the United Nations (UN) for help. The UN proposed to divide Palestine into two countries: one for the Jews and one for the Palestinians. The Palestinians rejected the proposal, and war broke out between the Jews and the Palestinians. The Jewish forces were victorious and occupied an even larger proportion of the land than they had originally been offered in the UN plan. The

British Mandate ended, and the state of Israel was declared in May 1948. The new state immediately faced a poorly coordinated attack by the armies of neighboring Arab Muslim states—Egypt, Lebanon, Syria, Transjordan (present-day Jordan), and Iraq—but Israel survived. During the conflict, around 726,000 Palestinians were forced to leave their homes or fled the new state in fear for their safety. The majority ended up in refugee camps in the West Bank under Jordanian rule or in the Egyptian-controlled Gaza Strip. More than one-fifth left Palestine altogether, most moving to neighboring Arab countries.

Since its establishment, Israel has been at war several times with its Arab neighbors. The Palestinian refugees have never given up the political struggle to regain their homeland. A minority have resorted to violent attacks, to which Israel has responded with force. In the 1980s, Islamic resistance movements developed in the Israeli-occupied West Bank and Gaza Strip. The largest movement, Hamas, adopted a mixture of social welfare measures and political and military struggle.

There have been attempts to achieve peace. In 1994, the Palestinian Authority (PA) was established. The PA had limited powers of self-government over the West Bank and Gaza Strip. In 2005, Israel withdrew its troops and Jewish settlers from the Gaza Strip, and the PA took over the territory. However, Palestinians maintained that the territory remained under effective Israeli military occupation, as did the West Bank. Hamas won the 2006 elections for the Palestinian Legislative Council (the Palestinian parliament). The governments of Europe, the U.S., and Israel saw this as a setback because of Hamas's refusal to recognize the right of Israel to exist and to give up armed resistance. They withdrew their economic support of the PA. As of mid-2006, progress toward a permanent peace treaty between Israel and the PA was stalled.

Islamic radicals Since World War II, there have been a number of Islamic movements within Muslim countries, pressing for a return to what they see as fundamental Islamic principles and a government based on sharia law. Most have been prepared to operate under existing governments, setting up mosques and welfare societies to show that Islam can work for the people. However, a minority of Islamic movements, such as some in Egypt and Algeria, have claimed that their countries are not truly Islamic and have used violence to try to take power.

These radical, or fundamentalist, Islamic resistance movements were inspired by the ideas of an Egyptian named Sayyid Qutb (1906–66). In 1952, Gamal Abdel Nasser seized power in Egypt and established a secular, or nonreligious, government. He persecuted the Muslim Brotherhood, and in 1956, Qutb was imprisoned for being a member of this organization. Qutb argued that although Nasser claimed he was a Muslim, the country was not ruled on an Islamic basis. In fact, he said Egypt was in a state of "barbarism," similar to pre-Islamic Arabia; therefore, Muslims were obligated to overthrow the government.

Qutb asked Muslims to model themselves after Muhammad. They should separate themselves from

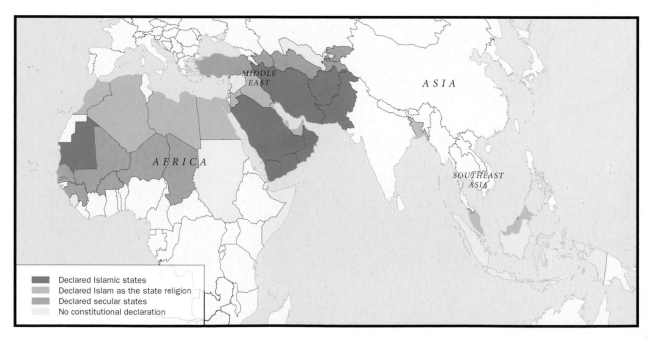

This map shows the traditionally Muslim countries of the world and indicates their relationship with Islam.

AFGHANISTAN

In 1979, the Soviet Union invaded Afghanistan, a Muslim country, in support of an unpopular Communist government that had taken power there. Muslim fighters, known as mujahideen, launched a jihad against the government and the Soviet forces. The mujahideen forced the Soviet troops out of Afghanistan in 1989. After several years of civil war, an extreme Islamic group called the Taliban took over the country in 1996. Under the Taliban, girls were not permitted to go to school and women were forbidden to go out to work. Harsh criminal punishments were imposed, including the amputation of a hand for theft. All forms of music, television, and sport were banned.

mainstream society and dedicate themselves to violent jihad. However, Muhammad actually preached a message of tolerance and opposed the use of force in religious matters. Qutb's ideas influenced all of the Sunni fundamentalist movements.

Iran In some countries, radical Islamic movements have succeeded in taking power. In Iran, Shah Mohammad Reza Pahlavi (ruled 1949–79) modernized the country economically, but no political parties were allowed, and his secret police crushed any opposition. A revolution in 1978–79 against the shah involved all sectors of society. After, a religious leader named Ayatollah Khomeini took power in Iran. He brought Islamic rule based on the Shia traditions of the country, that had remained strong under the influence of the ulema. Yet in a departure from traditional Shia doctrine, Khomeini declared that he alone would have absolute political and religious authority in Iran.

Khomeini greets a crowd in Qom, Iran, in December 1979. In that month, the people voted to create an Islamic Republic.

These women are enjoying a Ramadan celebration in a park in New York City. Most Muslims in non-Muslim lands want to be good citizens of their country while maintaining their traditions.

Under Khomeini, a strict Islamic code of dress and behavior was enforced: women had to wear the veil, alcohol and Western music were banned, and Islamic punishments were introduced. Khomeini imprisoned or killed all who opposed him.

Worldwide problems

Muslims have been affected by conflict in non-Muslim countries, too. In the 1990s and early 2000s, many Muslims around the world grew concerned about the suffering of people of their faith, such as the massacre of Muslims during the 1992–95 war in Bosnia (part of former Yugoslavia); the struggle in mainly Muslim Chechnya for independence from Russia; and the failure of the Palestinians to achieve an

independent state. In 2003, the U.S.-led war against Iraq and subsequent occupation of the country further inflamed Muslim feelings.

Many people tried to help their fellow Muslims by acts such as raising awareness of the issues and supporting Islamic charities working in war-torn regions. A small minority of Muslims turned to extreme methods. A radical Islamic movement called al Qaeda arose in the 1990s in response to the 1991 Gulf War against Iraq. The movement's spiritual leader was Osama bin Laden, who had been one of the leading figures within the mujahideen in Afghanistan during the 1980s. Those who supported al Qaeda resented eastern intervention in Muslim countries and were prepared to

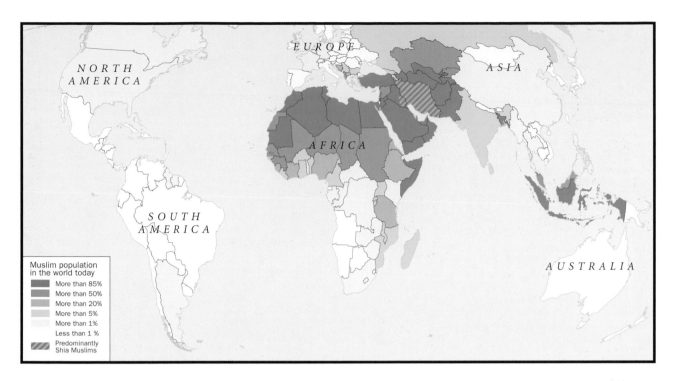

This map shows the distribution of Muslims in the world today.

Muslim population in the world today
- More than 85%
- More than 50%
- More than 20%
- More than 5%
- More than 1%
- Less than 1 %
- Predominantly Shia Muslims

fight Western interests through acts of terrorism. The most deadly terrorist attacks were the 9/11 attacks on New York City and Washington, D.C., of 2001, in which approximately 3,000 people were killed. There have been several other atrocities, including the killing of 202 people in Bali, Indonesia, in 2002 and bombings in Saudi Arabia, Morocco, Turkey, Egypt, Spain, and the United Kingdom.

Islam today Because of the minority of Muslims who commit acts of terrorism, there is a growing mistrust of Muslims in general among many Western countries. Non-Muslims may see the Islamic faith as intolerant and violent. However, the majority of Muslims condemn terrorism and seek a peaceful resolution to conflict.

Islam has had a significant worldwide influence over the past 1,400 years. Beginning with one man in the seventh-century Arabian desert, it is now a thriving religion with 1.3 billion followers living in more than 200 countries. Islam will clearly remain a religion of major significance in the twenty-first century.

Yusuf Abdallah al-Qaradawi (born 1926)

A popular Muslim scholar and writer living in Qatar, al-Qaradawi is widely regarded among Muslims as a leader of moderate Islam. Conservative Muslims regard him as too liberal in his beliefs, while many Western critics regard him as a dangerous radical who supports violent struggle to further the cause of Islam. For example, he believes that Palestinian suicide bomb attacks on Israeli civilians are an acceptable form of resistance to Israel. However, Al-Qaradawi has argued in favor of democracy for Muslim countries, saying that Islam grants people the right to choose their ruler and argues for tolerance among Muslims. In 2004, he announced the formation of the International Association of Muslim Scholars (IAMS) "with the aim of preserving Islamic identity, promoting religious awareness, confronting 'destructive [extremist] trends,' and giving advice to leaders of Muslim countries." Al-Qaradawi said, "IAMS will open up to other religions and cultures as it firmly believes in the importance of promoting dialogue with the other."

GREAT LIVES

Muhammad (570–632 CE)

The Prophet Muhammad was born in the city of Mecca. After receiving revelations for two years, he preached a message of social justice and the worship of one true God. The new religion became known as Islam. Muhammad and his followers migrated to the city of Medina in 622, where they established a community. By the time of the Prophet's death, Medina had become the center of a growing Islamic community.

Ali Ibn Abu Talib (ca. 600–661)

Ali was taken into Muhammad's care as a child. He was one of the first converts to Islam and a devoted follower of the Prophet. Ali married Muhammad's daughter Fatimah and they had two sons, Hasan and Hussain. Following the murder of the caliph Uthman in 656, Ali became caliph. However, his rule was opposed by Muawiya, who by 660 had seized Egypt and the Hejaz in western Arabia from Ali's control. In 661, Ali was murdered by a Kharijite. Ali is regarded by the Shia as the true successor of Muhammad.

Hasan al-Basri (642–728)

Hasan al-Basri was brought up in Medina. In 658, he moved to Basra (in modern-day Iraq) where he became a well-known preacher. He began a religious reform movement that encouraged followers to meditate on the Qur'an and surrender to God's will in order to become truly happy. He lived a frugal life and was critical of the luxury of the Umayyad court, although he did not oppose the dynasty's rule. Later Muslims remembered al-Basri for his strongly held religious values and self-discipline, and Sufis held him to be their first spiritual master.

Muhammad ibn Abd al-Wahhab (1703–92)

Born to a devout family, al-Wahhab studied in Medina with the followers of Shah Wali Allah. He then lived in Basra and, subsequently, Iran. In 1736, he began to preach against Sufi and Shia practices and argued that the Islamic community should return to the purity of seventh-century Islam. He returned to Arabia in 1744, where he made an alliance with Ibn Saud, the ruler of Najd (in modern-day Saudi Arabia). Together they initiated a campaign of conquest in Arabia. By 1800, al-Wahhab's religious ideas were dominant in the Arabian Peninsula.

Muhammad Abduh (1849–1905)

As a young man, Muhammad Abduh attended al-Azhar University in Cairo, Egypt. In 1872, he came under the influence of Jamal al-Din al-Afghani. In 1882, he took part in a rebellion against British control of Egypt for which he was exiled. Allowed to return in 1888, he became a judge, and in 1899, a mufti (Islamic legal counselor). Abduh introduced several legal reforms that promoted fairness, welfare, and common sense, even if this meant occasionally disregarding the Qur'an. After his death, he became widely known as the father of the Islamic reform movement.

Hasan al-Banna (1906–49)

Born in Egypt, al-Banna went to Cairo in 1923 to pursue a degree in education. In 1927, he became a schoolteacher in Ismailia near the Suez Canal. The following year, he established the Muslim Brotherhood. In the 1930s, al-Banna moved to Cairo for a teaching position. The Muslim Brotherhood grew rapidly and became a powerful political force, working to achieve change through religious revival and welfare work. Many members came to believe that the Egyptian government did not act in the interests of the people. After World War II, al-Banna could no longer control the movement; some members turned to violent methods and became involved in the assassination of political figures. Al-Banna was assassinated himself in 1949.

Sayyid Qutb (1906–66)

In his early life, Qutb admired Western culture and secular politics. But after living in the U.S. from 1948 to

1950, he expressed disapproval of the freedom of women and the racism he encountered there. On his return to Egypt, he joined the Muslim Brotherhood, who helped bring Nasser to power in 1952. The Muslim Brotherhood hoped that Nasser would rule according to Islamic traditions. Qutb still believed that Western democracy could be combined with Islam, but the Muslim Brotherhood increasingly clashed with Nasser's secular government. In 1954, after an attempt to assassinate Nasser, the Muslim Brotherhood was banned. Qutb was sent to prison in 1956, and in 1966, he was executed for an alleged plot to overthrow Nasser. Qutb wrote several books, including *Milestones* (published in 1964), in which he argued that a revolution was needed to bring about the establishment of a true Islamic state ruled by God and sharia law. His ideas had a significant influence on later Sunni Islamic fundamentalist movements.

Ayatollah Ruhollah Khomeini (ca. 1900–89)

The son of a Shia religious leader in Iran, the young Khomeini was educated in various religious schools. He became a Shia scholar, teacher, and a forceful opponent of Iran's ruler, Shah Mohammad Reza Pahlavi. In the 1950s, Khomeini became an ayatollah, a major religious leader, and by the 1960s, he was appointed a grand ayatollah—one of the supreme religious leaders. He was exiled for his anti-government activity in 1964 and lived abroad until his triumphant return to Iran in February 1979 following the departure of the shah. In December 1979, Iran was declared an Islamic Republic, and Khomeini appointed himself political and religious leader for life.

FACTS AND FIGURES

The world's Muslim population (mid-2005)

Africa	357,846,000
Asia	910,375,000
Europe	33,303,000
South America	1,745,000
North America	5,259,000
Oceania	412,000
World	1,308,941,000
Muslims as a percentage of members of all religions worldwide	20.3
Number of countries where Muslims live	206

Source: Encyclopedia Britannica, 2006

List of holy sites

Ajmer, Rajasthan, India	(page 23)
Al-Aqsa Mosque, Jerusalem, Israel	(page 36)
Ayodhya Mosque (destroyed), northern India	(page 35)
Dome of the Rock, Jerusalem, Israel	(page 9)
Haram al-Sharif, Jerusalem, Israel	(page 36)
Jama Masjid, Delhi, India	(page 24)
Medina, Arabia	(page 6)
Mecca, Arabia	(page 5)
Karbala, Iraq	(page 8)
Mosque of Süleyman, Istanbul, Turkey	(page 21)

Calendar of festivals and holy days

There are 12 lunar months in the Muslim calendar: Muharram, Safar, Rabi al-Awwal, Rabi al-Thani, Jumada al-Awwal, Jumada al-Thani, Rajab, Shaban, Ramadan, Shawwal, Dhul al-Qidah, and Dhul al-Hijjah. Each new month begins with the new moon. A lunar year is about 11 days shorter that the standard 365-day year. This means that events in the Islamic year move back in the standard calendar, year by year.

Month and date	Event	What happens
Muharram 1	Hegira, the Islamic New Year	Celebration of the hegira (migration) to Medina.
Muharram 1–10	Ashura	Muslims, especially the Shia, remember the death of Hussain.
Rabi al-Awwal 12–17	Milad an-Nabi (Birth of the Prophet)	Celebrations of the life of the Prophet and reading of the Sira, his biography.
Jumada al-Thani 20	Yawm al-Zahrah (Birthday of Fatimah Zahrah, daughter of the Prophet)	Shia Muslims tell stories about Fatimah's life. It is Women's Day in Iran.
Rajab 27	Lailat ul-Miraj	Celebration of Muhammad's rise to heaven, during which God told him Muslims should pray five times a day.
Shaban 14–15	Lailat ul-Barat	The Night of Forgiveness, when people are forgiven their sins.
Ramadan	The month of fasting	Muslims fast each day from dawn to sunset.
Ramadan 27	Lailat ul-Qadr	People remember the night when the first part of the Qur'an was revealed to Muhammad.
Shawwal 1	Id ul-Fitr	Festival to mark the end of Ramadan. Muslims give zakat.
Dhul al-Hijjah 8–10	The Hajj	At least once in their lifetime, Muslims make the pilgrimage to the holy sites in Arabia.
Dhul al-Hijjah 10–12	Id ul-Adha	A feast is held to remember how God tested Abraham's faith by asking him to sacrifice his son Ishmael.

FURTHER INFORMATION

Books

Beliefs and Cultures: Muslim by R. Tames (Franklin Watts, 2004)

Examining Religions: Islam by Ruqaiyyah Waris Maqsood (Heinemann, 1995)

Great Religious Leaders: Muhammad and Islam by Kerena Marchant (Hodder Wayland, 2005)

History in Art: Islamic Empires by Nicola Barber (Raintree, 2005)

Oxford Dictionary of Islam by John L. Esposito (Oxford University Press, USA, 2004)

Religion in Focus: Islam by Geoff Teece (Franklin Watts, 2003)

Religious Lives: Muhammad and Islam by Ruth Nason (Hodder Wayland, 2006)

World Faiths: Islam by Trevor Barnes (Kingfisher, 2005)

Books for older readers and resources for teachers

No God but God by Reza Aslan (Arrow, 2006)

Historical Atlas of the Islamic World by David Nicolle (Mercury Books, 2004)

Islam: Religion, History, and Civilization by Seyyed Hossein Nasr (HarperSanFrancisco, 2002)

Islam: A Short History by Karen Armstrong (Modern Library, 2002)

Web sites

www.channel4.com/science/microsites/S/science/society/islamicscience.html
A UK site that looks at the Islamic contributions to science.

www.islamicity.com/education/
Islamicity contains sections on religion and Islamic history, culture, and science.

http://www.pbs.org/empires/islam/index.html
A companion site to the PBS program "Islam: Empire of Faith" providing highlights of Islam's long history and rich culture.

TIME LINE

610 The Prophet Muhammad begins to receive revelations of the Qur'an in Mecca.

622 The Prophet and his followers make the hegira to Yathrib (Medina).

630 Muhammad takes over Mecca.

632 Death of the Prophet.

632–661 Rule of the first four caliphs: Abu Bakr, Umar ibn al-Khattab, Uthman ibn Affan, and Ali ibn Abi Talib.

661–750 Rule of the Umayyad dynasty.

711 Islam first appears in India.

750–1258 Rule of the Abbasid dynasty; from 940, the Abbasid caliphs have only symbolic authority.

756 Abd ar-Rahman establishes the Caliphate of Córdoba in Spain.

909–1171 The Shia Fatimids rule in North Africa.

990–1118 Rule of the Seljuk Empire, which at its greatest extent stretches from Rum (modern-day Turkey) in the west to Transoxiana (present-day Uzbekistan and parts of Turkmenistan and Kazakstan) in the east.

1099 The crusaders conquer Jerusalem and establish four crusader states in Palestine, Anatolia, and Syria.

1187 Saladin recaptures Jerusalem and founds the Ayyubid dynasty, which rules Egypt, part of modern-day Iraq, most of Syria, and Yemen.

1250 The Mamluk dynasty defeats the Ayyubids and rules Egypt and Syria until 1517.

1256–1335 The Mongols rule Iran and modern-day Iraq.

1258 The Mongols defeat the Abbasids and sack Baghdad.

1369–1405 Timur reverses the decline in the Mongol Empire, but it falls apart after his death.

1453 The Ottoman sultan Mehmet II conquers Constantinople and ends the Byzantine Empire.

1502 Shah Ismail founds the Safavid dynasty, which lasts until 1736.

1524 The first major Muslim state in Southeast Asia is established in Aceh.

1526 Babur, the first Mogul emperor, conquers Delhi.

1556–1605 Akbar extends Mogul power over most of the Indian subcontinent.

1739 Nadir Shah invades northern India and sacks Delhi.

1779 The Qajar dynasty takes power in Iran.

1808 The Sokoto Caliphate is formed in modern-day northern Nigeria.

1857 The Indian Revolt against the British in India.

1882 The British take control of Egypt.

1928 Hasan al-Banna establishes the Muslim Brotherhood in Egypt.

1932 The Kingdom of Saudi Arabia is established.

1947 India gains independence and the country is partitioned between mainly Hindu India and mainly Muslim Pakistan.

1948 The State of Israel is established, and around three-quarters of a million mostly Muslim Palestinians flee.

1952 Gamal Abdel Nasser seizes power in Egypt.

1967 The entire city of Jerusalem comes under Israeli control.

1979 A revolution in Iran leads to Islamic rule by Ayatollah Khomeini.

1979 The Soviet Union takes over Afghanistan; Muslim mujahideen wage jihad against Soviet power.

1989 The mujahideen force the Soviet army out of Afghanistan.

1990 Iraq occupies Kuwait.

1991 The U.S. leads the Gulf War against Iraq.

1996 The Taliban take power in Afghanistan.

2001 Terrorist attacks on the U.S.

2003 The U.S. leads a war against Iraq.

GLOSSARY

Allah The Arabic word for God.

ayatollah A senior Shia religious leader.

Byzantine Empire A Christian empire centered around Constantinople (in present-day Turkey) that lasted from 330 CE to 1453.

caliph A ruler of the Muslim community. The title was used by the first four successors to Muhammad and by the Umayyads, Abbasids, Mamluks, and Ottomans.

caliphate The lands and peoples ruled by a caliph.

caste system The system in Hindu society that divides people into four different classes.

colonize Take control of an area or a country that is not your own, especially using force.

Communism The system of government in the former Soviet Union, in which the state controlled all property and the means of producing goods, such as factories and farms.

Crusades Christian military expeditions, especially in the eleventh to the thirteenth centuries, which tried to regain the Holy Land of Palestine from the Muslims.

deity A god or goddess in a religion that worships many gods.

democracy A system of government in which the people of a country can vote to elect their representatives.

dynasty A series of rulers of a country who all belong to the same family.

Fulani A people of West Africa who lived a nomadic lifestyle, moving from place to place to graze their animals.

fundamentalism The practice of strictly following the basic rules and teachings of a religion.

Hadith The written record of the teachings and actions of Muhammad that was compiled by his close companions and members of his family.

hajj The religious journey to Mecca and the other holy sites of Arabia that Muslims try to make at least once in their lifetime.

hegira Also called hijra; the migration of the Prophet Muhammad and the first Muslim community from Mecca to Medina in 622 CE.

Imam The leader of the Muslim community. Most Shia Muslims use the title for the 12 descendants of the Prophet through Ali ibn Abi Talib and Fatimah, whom they considered to be the true rulers of the Muslims. Some Shia believe there were just seven Imams. The word *imam* is used in modern times to refer to the prayer leader of a mosque and leader of a local Muslim community.

interest The extra money that people have to pay back when they repay money they have borrowed.

jihad Struggle on behalf of God and Islam. It refers to the effort of individual Muslims to improve themselves and their community, as well as a war waged to defend Islam.

khan The leader of a Mongol tribe. The Great Khan (Genghis Khan, for example) was the supreme leader.

Kharijites A radical sect that broke away from supporting Ali during his caliphate.

Kurdish From a region in the Middle East that includes part of modern Turkey, Iran, Iraq, Syria, Armenia, and Azerbaijan, the Kurds were a mostly Muslim people who kept livestock for a living.

madrassa An Islamic religious school.

Mahdi The "hidden imam," who some Muslims believe will return someday and will bring justice to the world.

mamluk Slaves bought by Muslim rulers in the Middle Ages to fight in their armies. A few freed mamluks rose in society to become rulers.

nationalist A person in a country ruled by a foreign state who wants his or her country to be independent.

pasha A person of high rank in the Ottoman Empire; the title was usually given to governors and generals.

pir A sufi leader.

qadi A judge who administers sharia law.

Qur'an The Muslim holy book.

Ramadan The month in the Islamic calendar during which Muslims fast each day from dawn until sunset.

revelations In Islam, divine messages that were passed on through the Prophet Muhammad and gave guidance to people on how to live their lives.

robai A form of Persian poetry made up of verses of four lines

sack Raid, loot, and destroy a town.

Sasanian Empire An Iranian dynasty that began in the third century A.D. and was defeated by Arab Muslims between 637 and 651.

shah King of Iran.

shahadah The Muslim declaration of faith in Allah.

sharia The body of Islamic holy laws that come mostly from the Qur'an and Hadith.

Shia Muslims Muslims who believe that Ali should have ruled after Muhammad; most honor a number of Imams, direct descendants of Ali and Fatimah, the Prophet's daughter.

Soviet Union A country formed from the territories of the Russian Empire in 1917, which lasted until 1991.

Sufism The mystical traditions of Islam.

sultan A Muslim ruler.

sultanate The land ruled by a sultan.

Sunna The habits and religious practice of Muhammad, which were recorded by his family and companions. The Sunna forms part of Islamic law and is regarded as the Islamic ideal for Muslims to follow.

Sunni Muslims The term for the majority of Muslims, who honor the four caliphs that followed Muhammad.

Syriac The language of ancient Syria.

ulema The Islamic clergy: the learned religious men who are the guardians of the legal and religious traditions of Islam.

Umma The Muslim community in Medina; as Islam spread, also used to mean the Muslim community as a whole.

United Nations (UN) An international organization to which most of the world's countries belong. The UN aims to improve economic and social conditions and to solve political problems in the world through peaceful means.

zakat The tax that all Muslims pay each year to help the poor.

Zoroastrianism A religion of ancient Persia based on one supreme god.

INDEX